I0511776

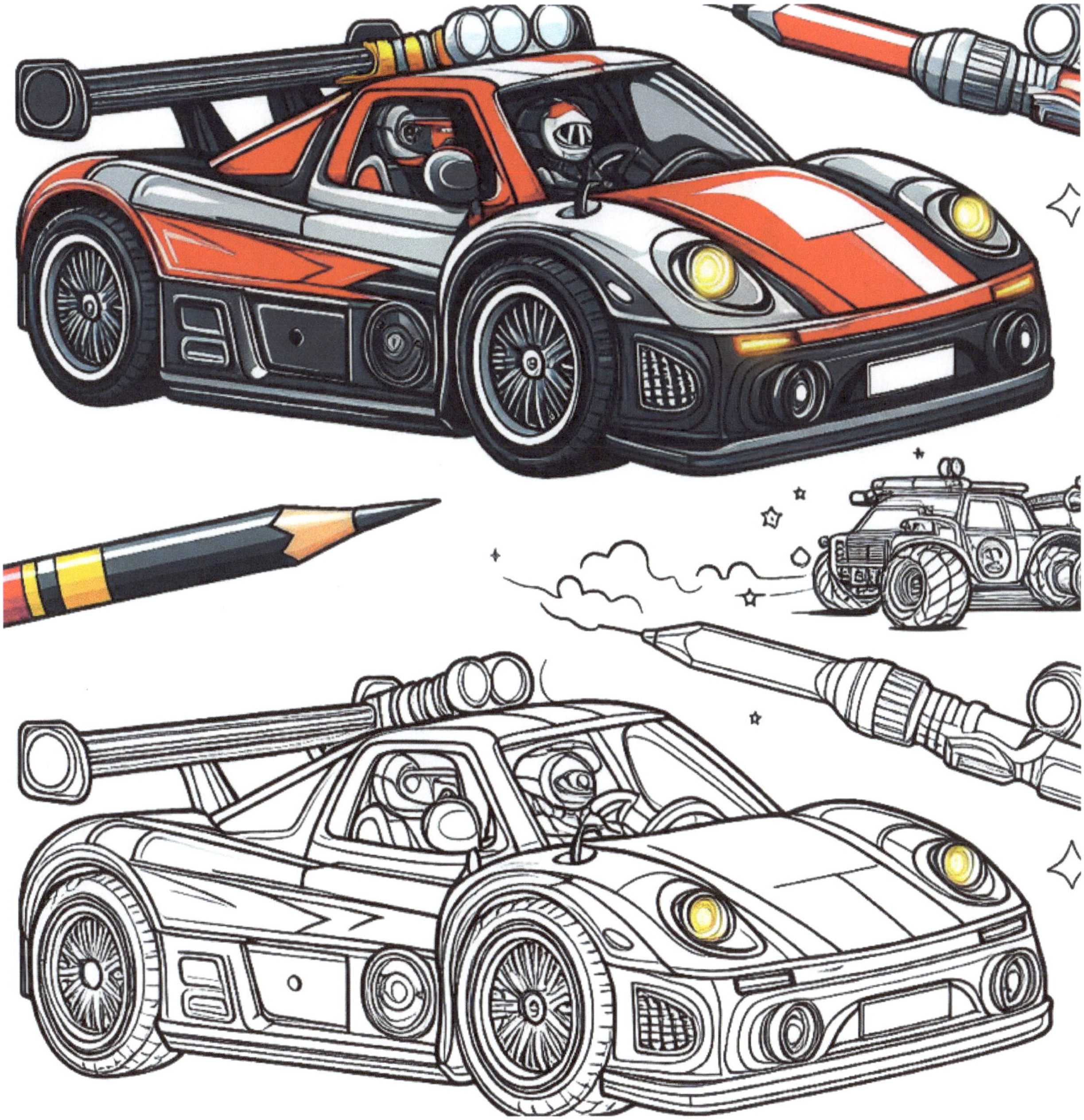

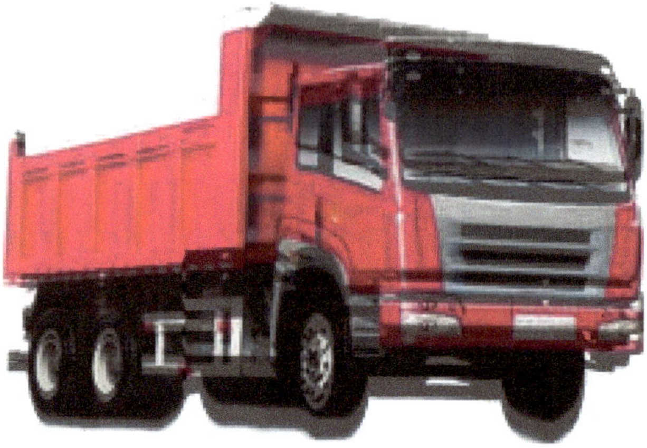

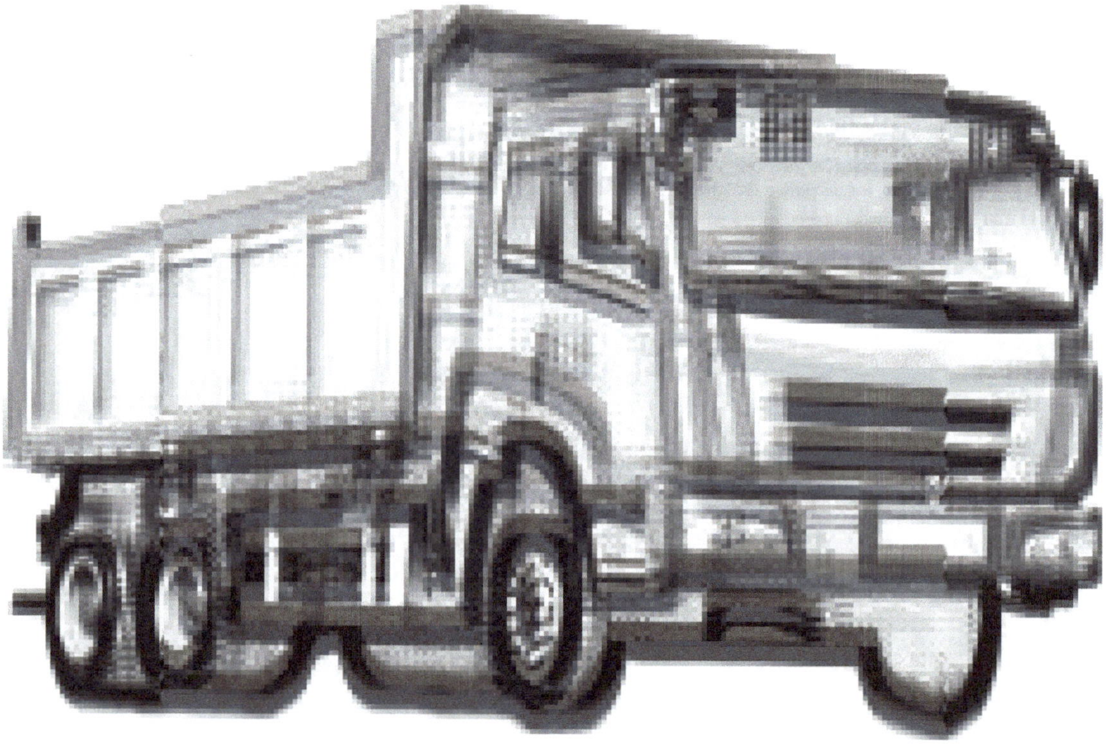

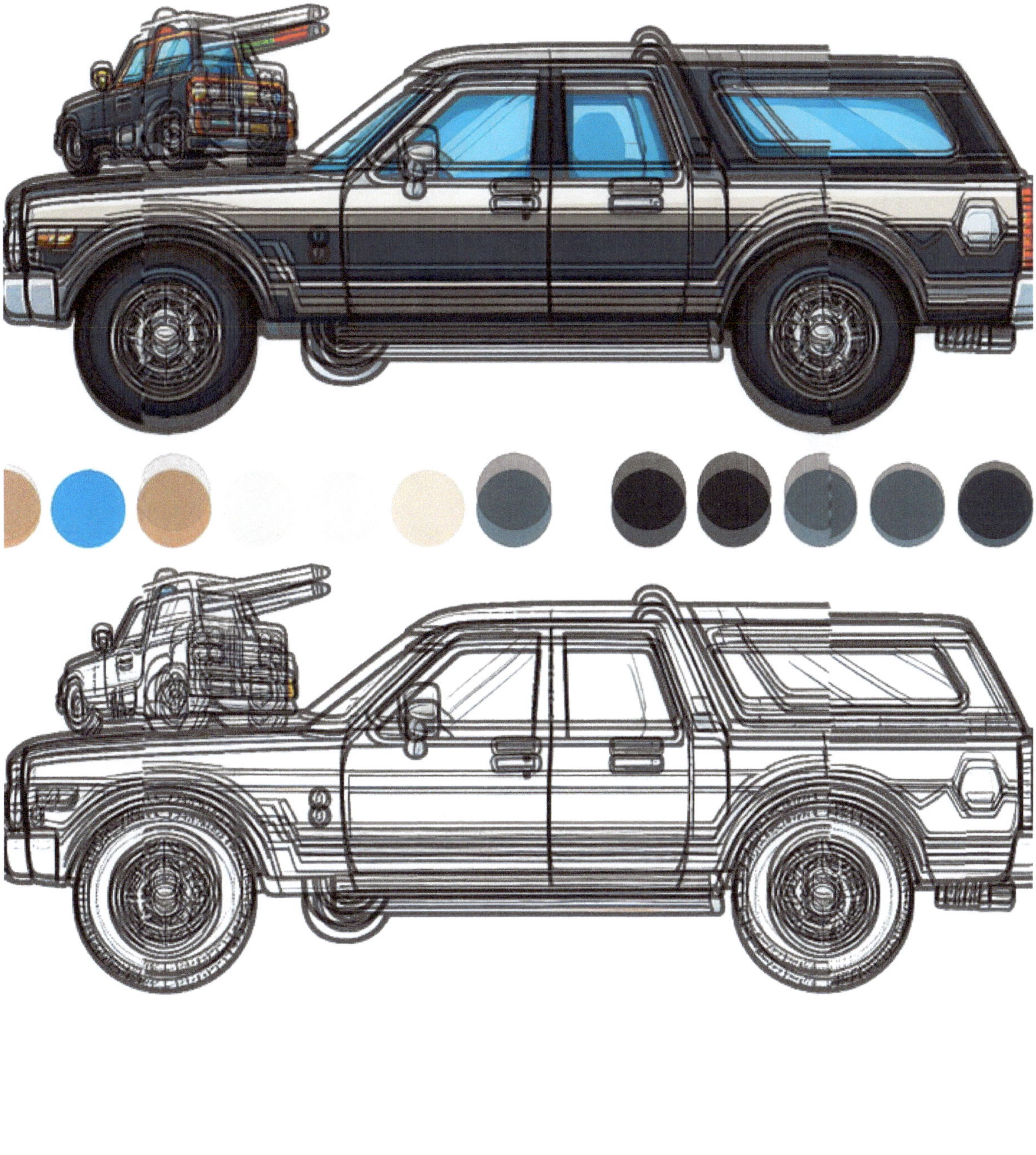

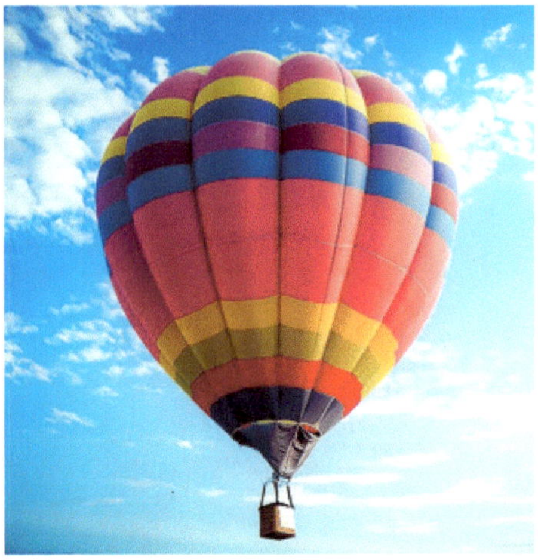

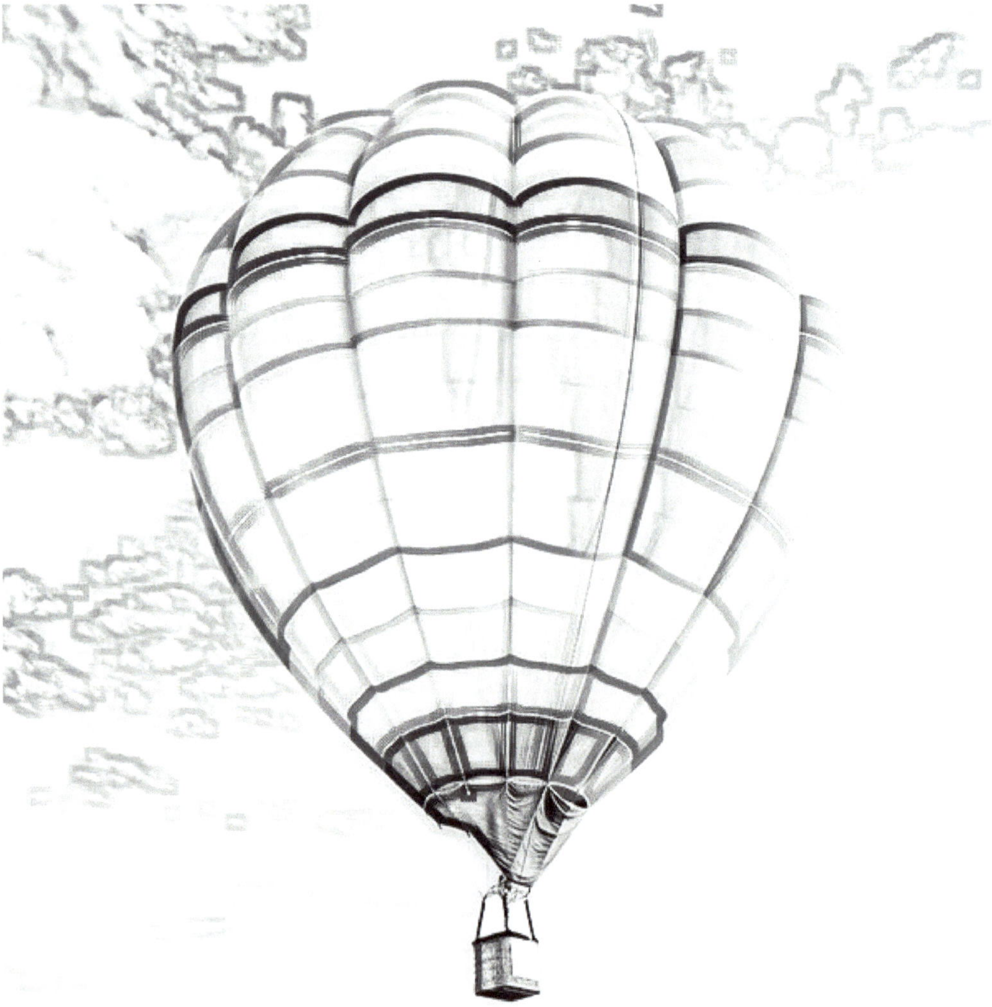

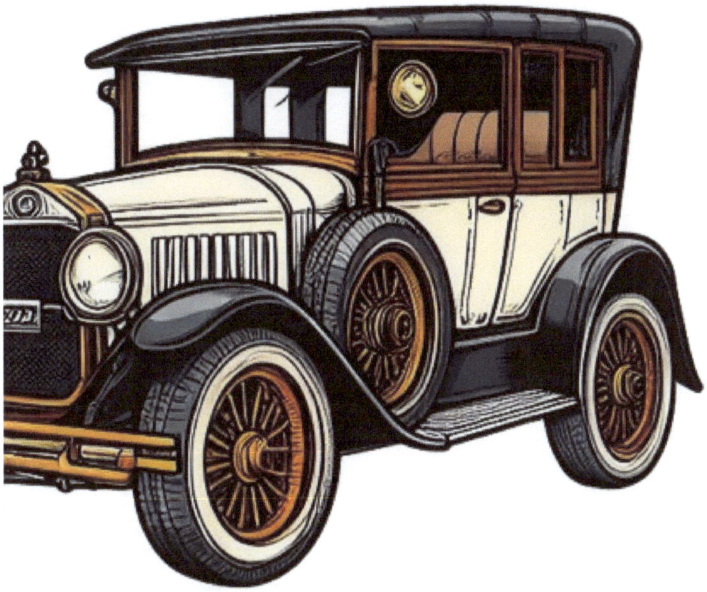

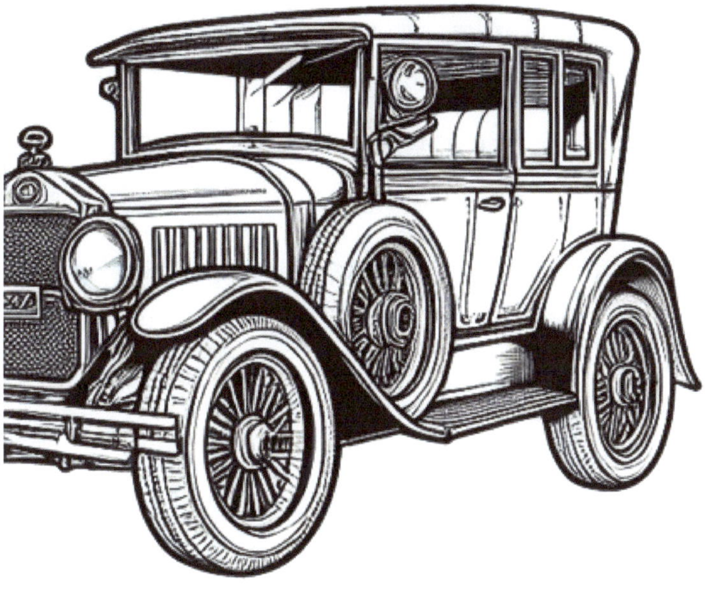

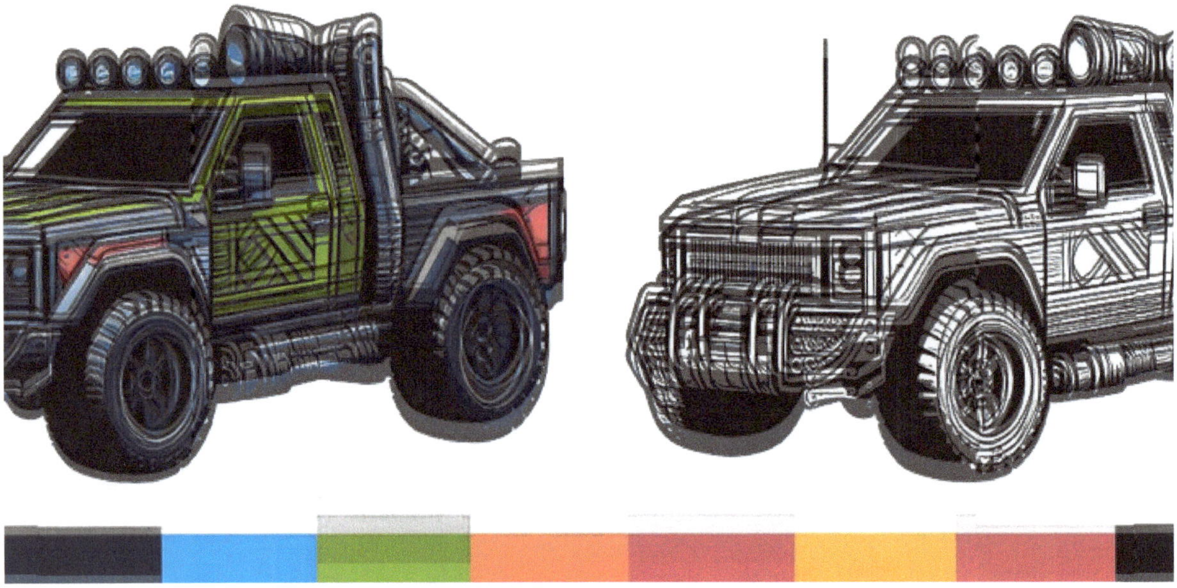

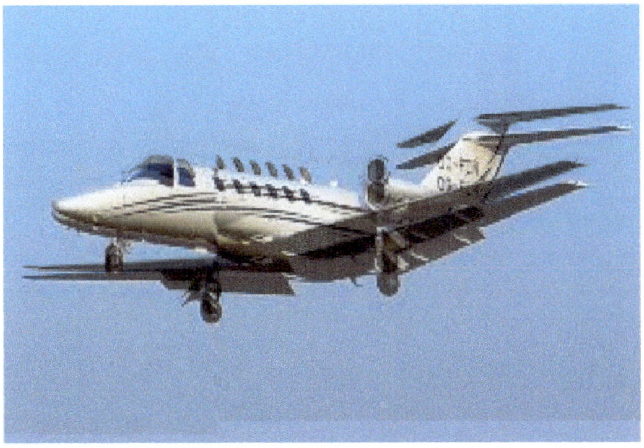

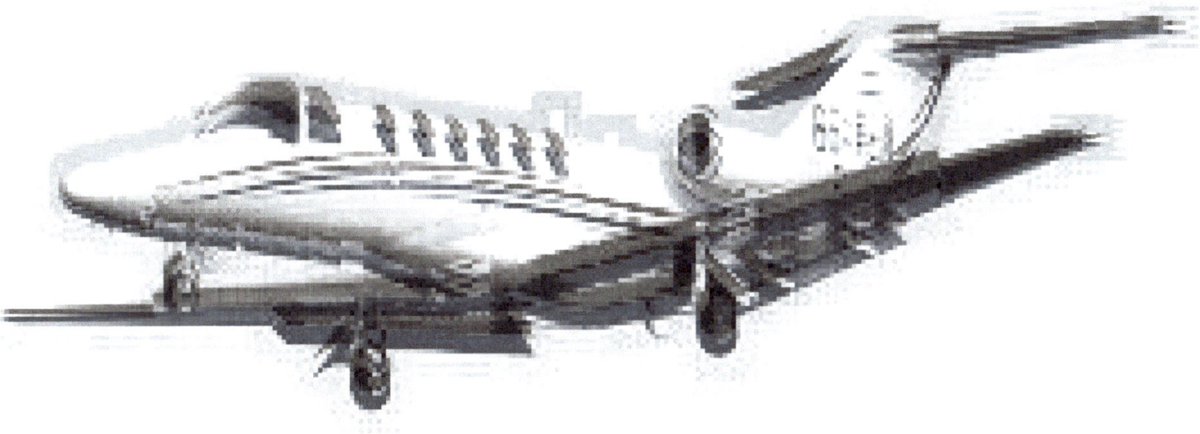

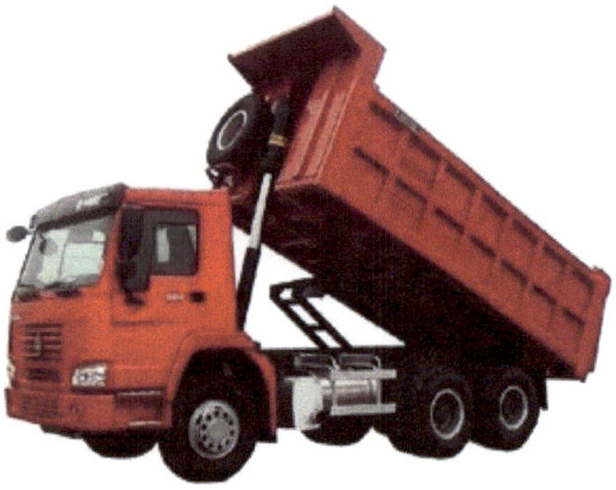

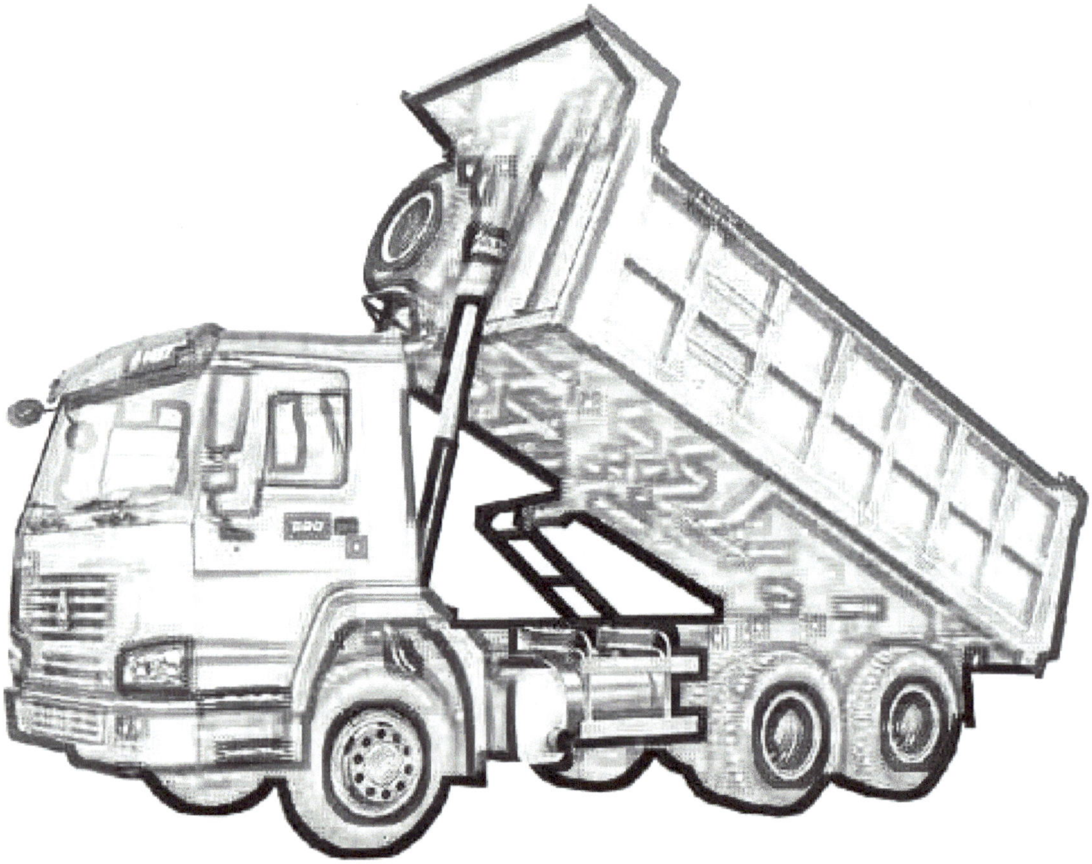

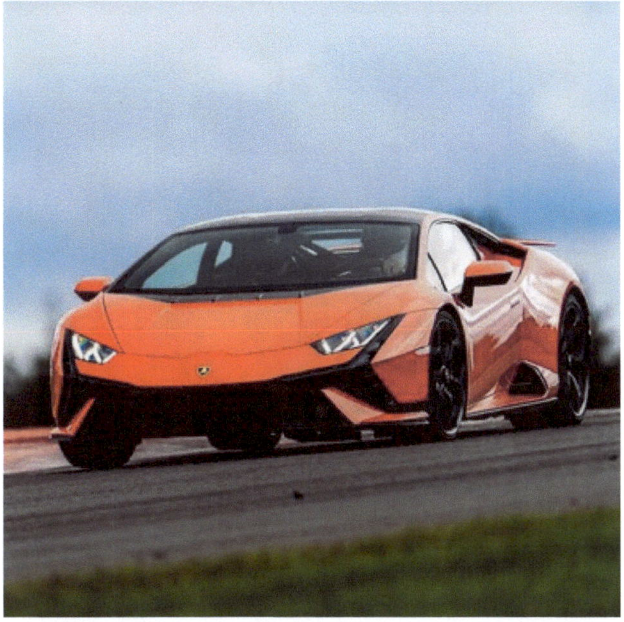

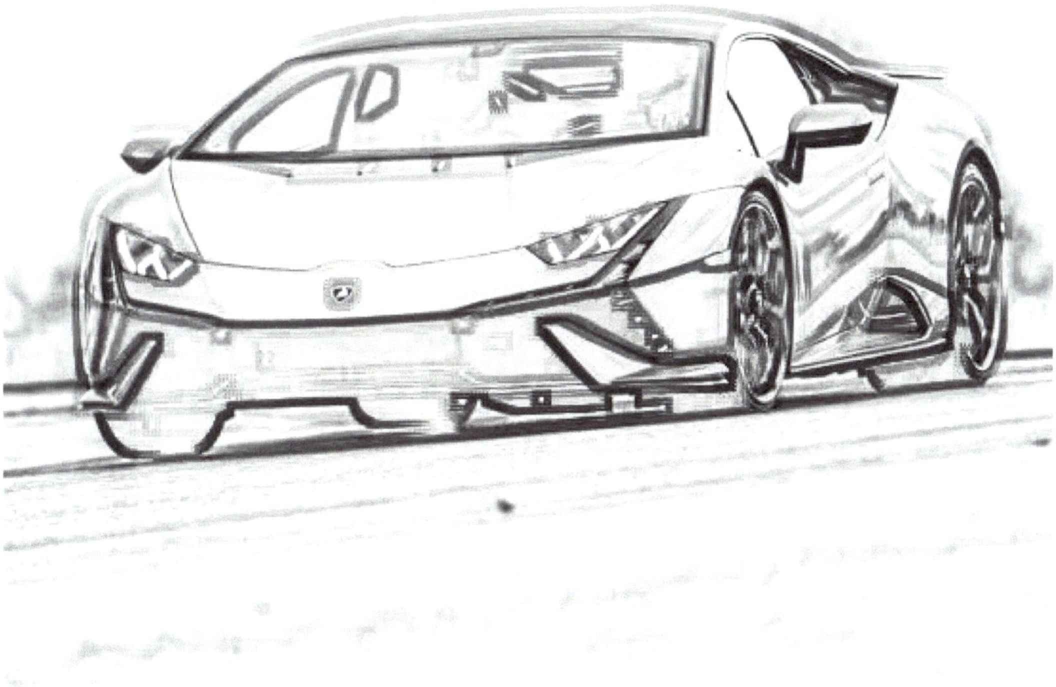

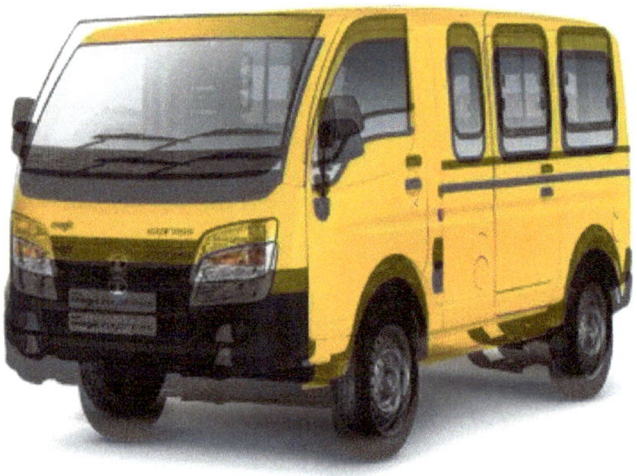

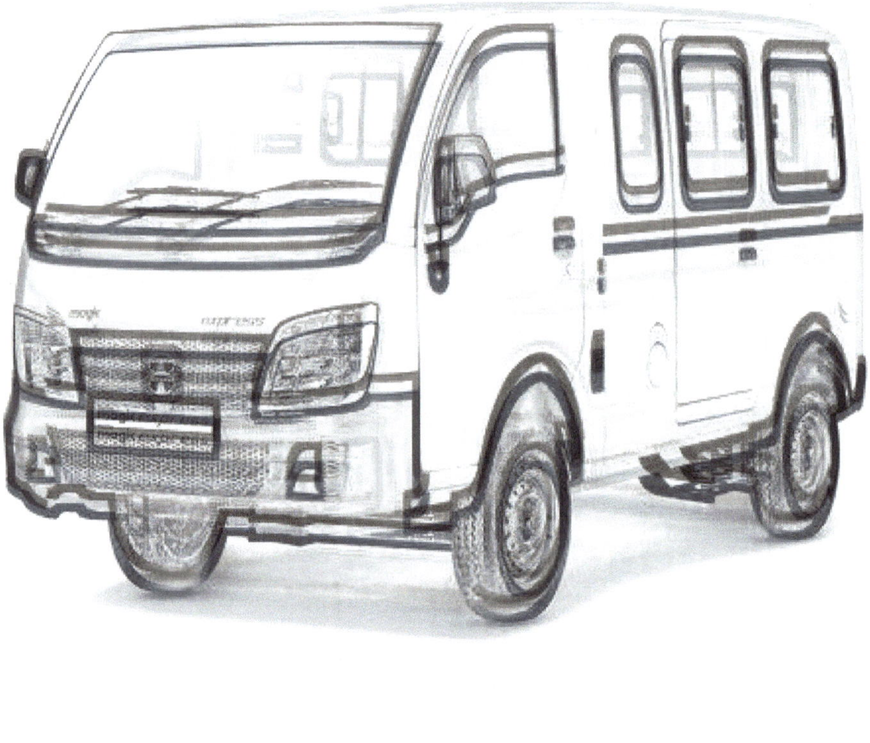

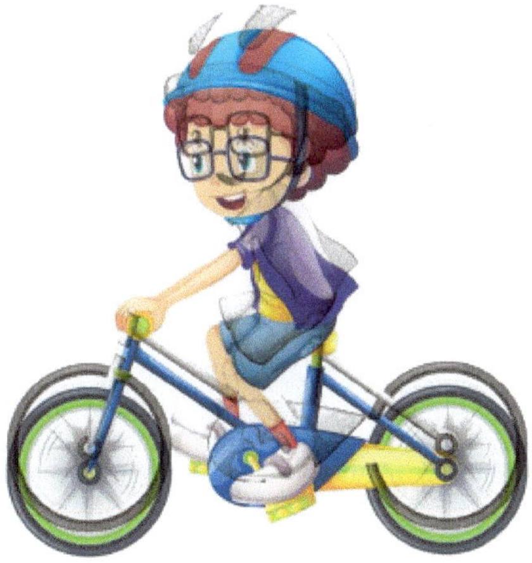

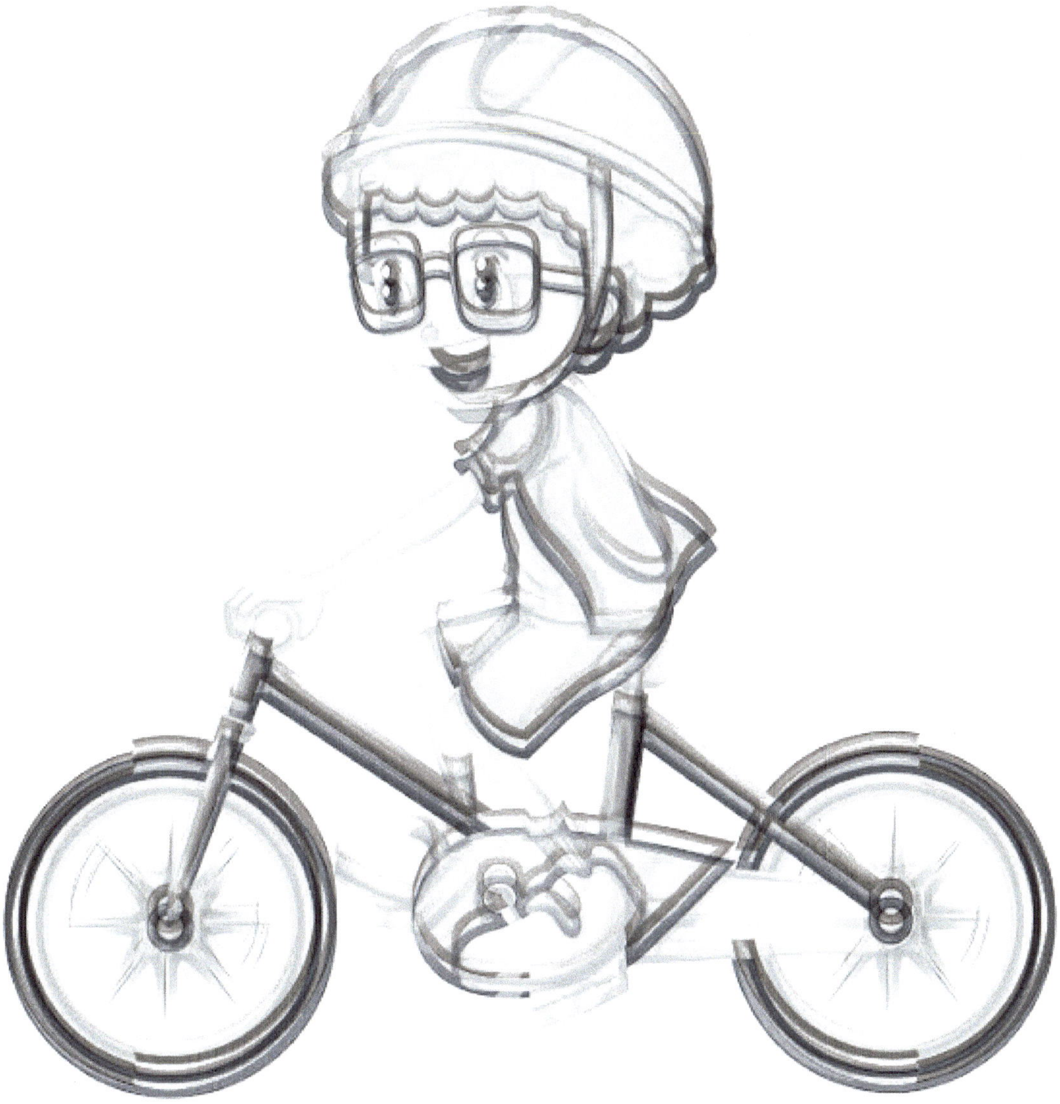

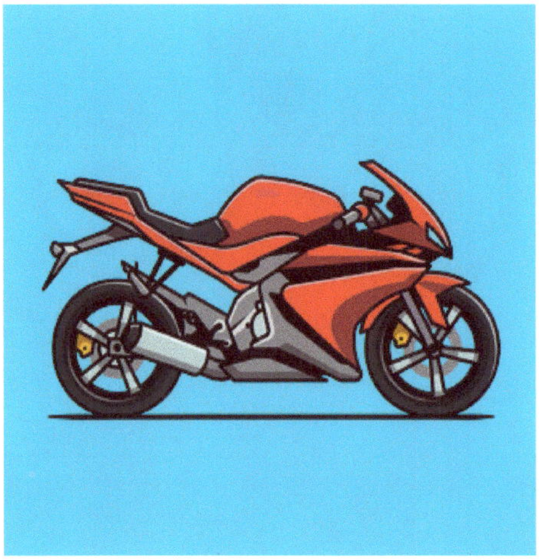

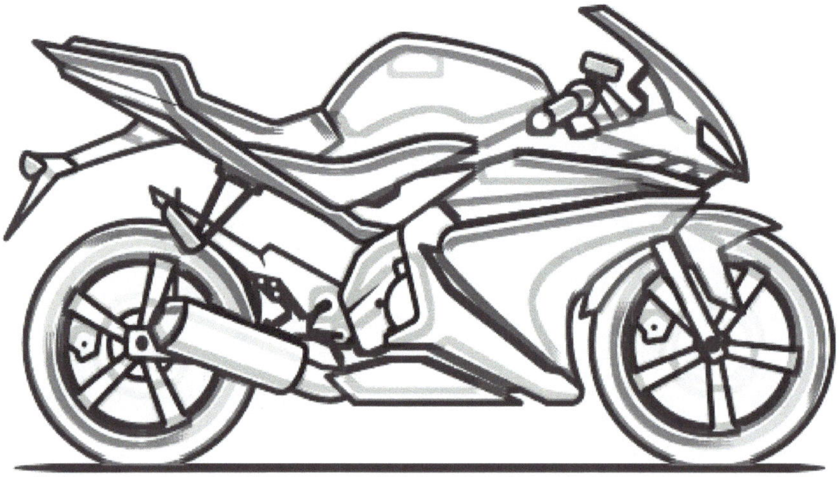

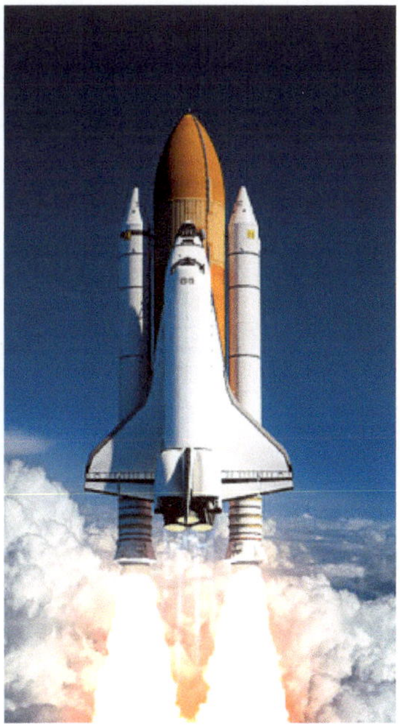

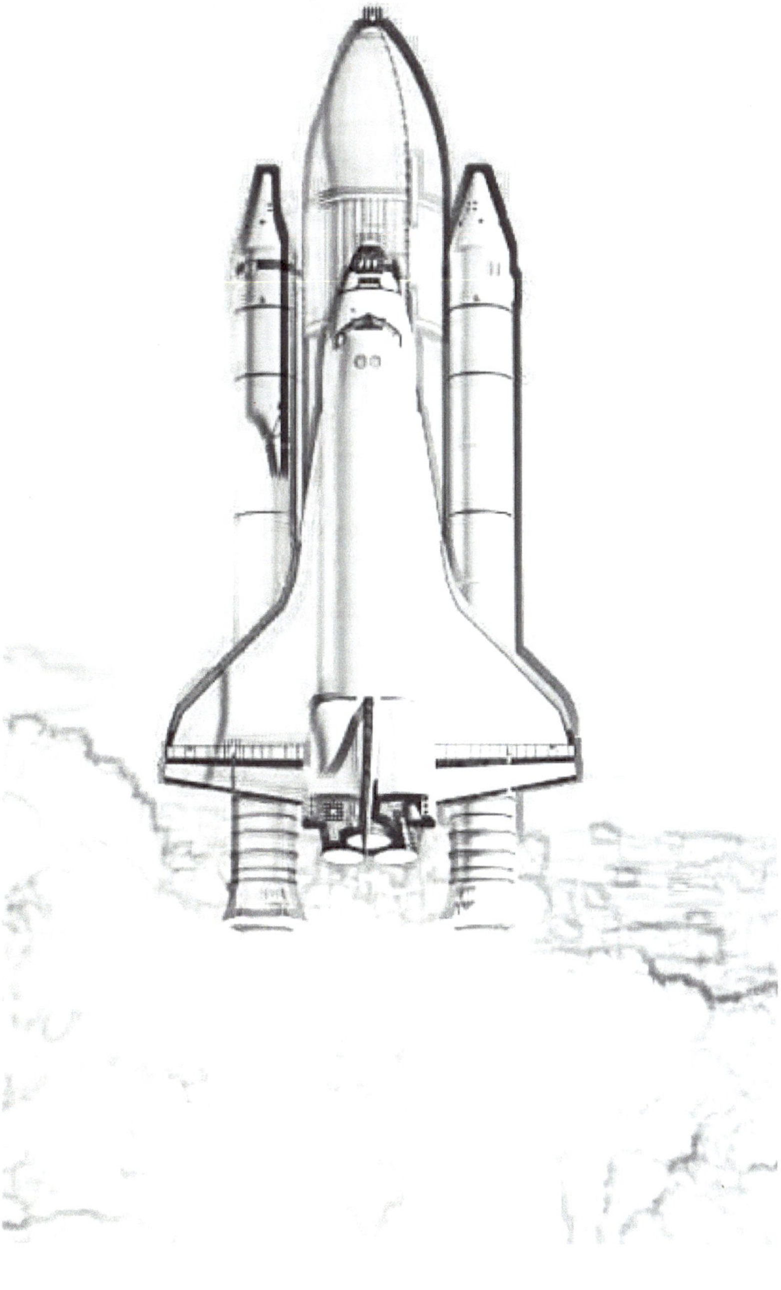

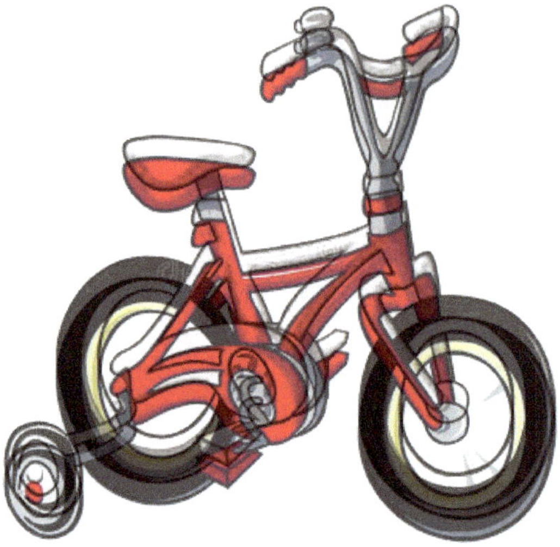

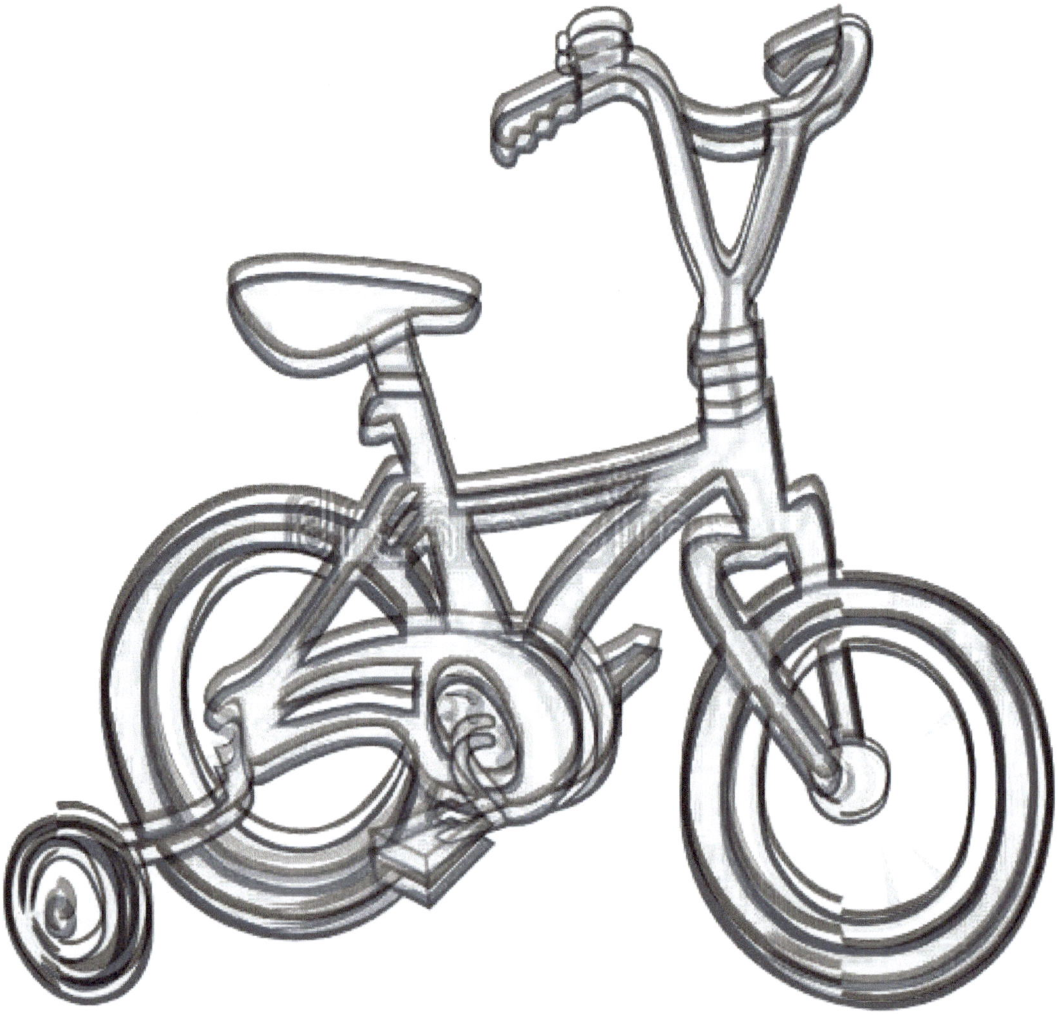

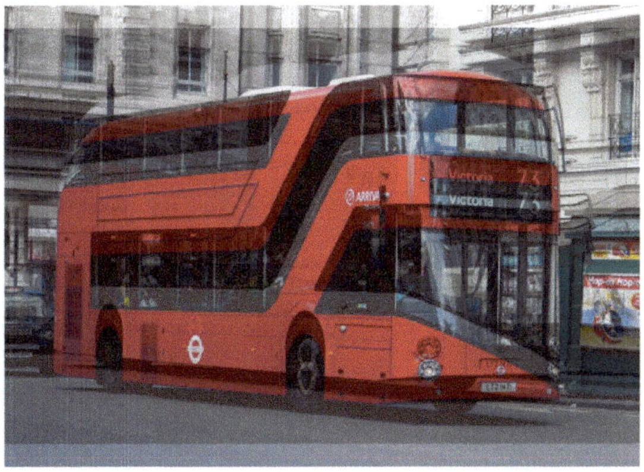
Victoria 73

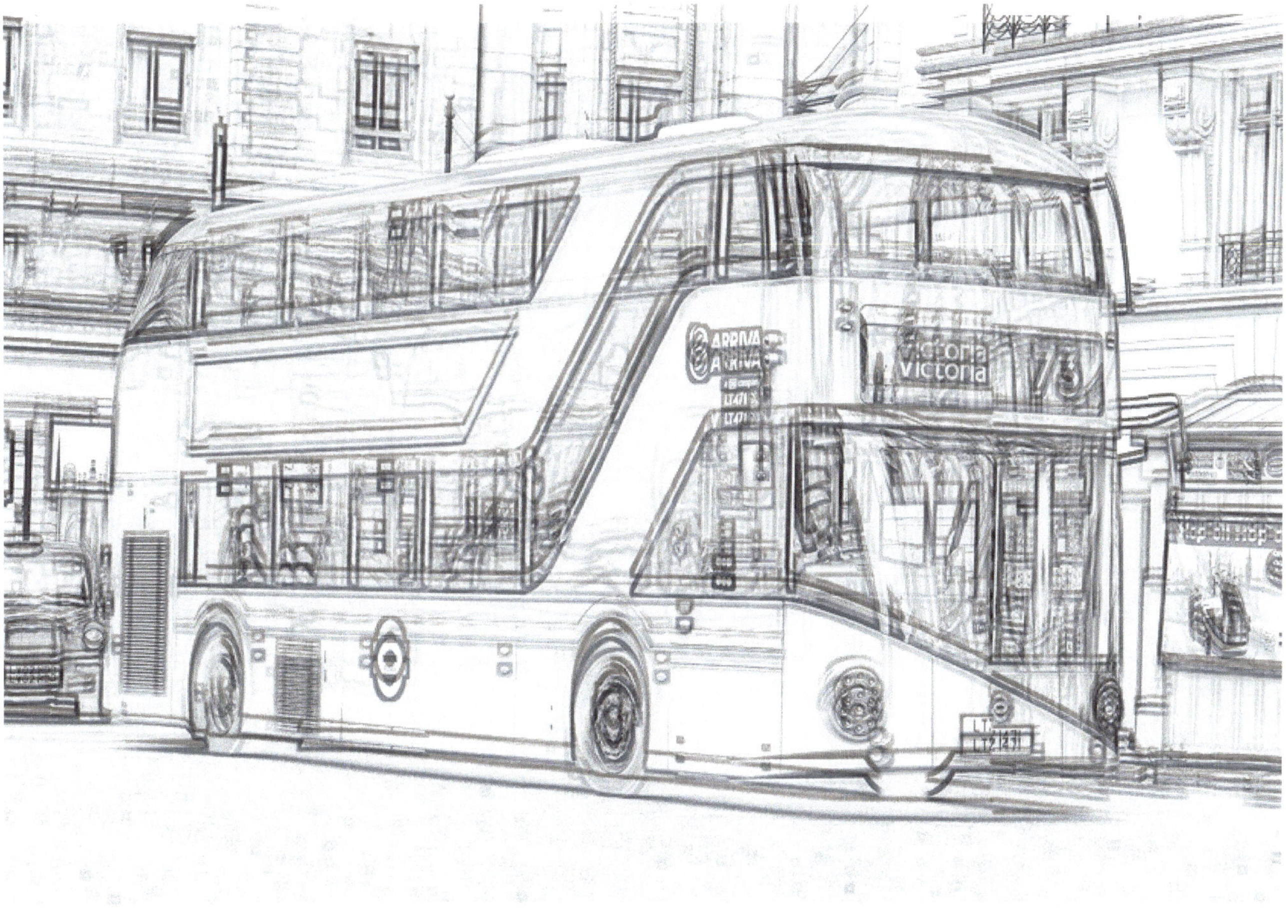
ARRIVA
Victoria
73

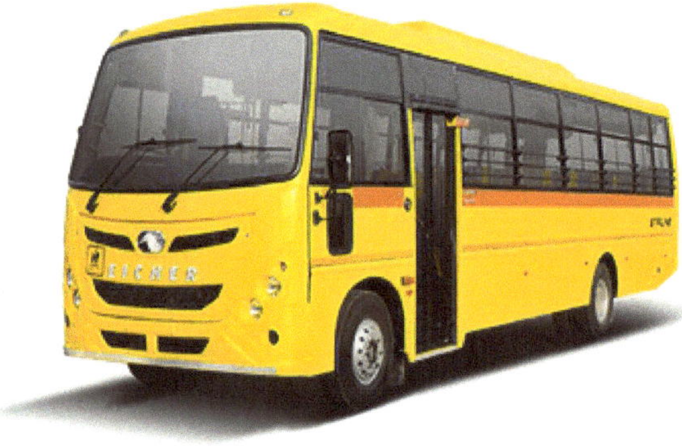
EICHER

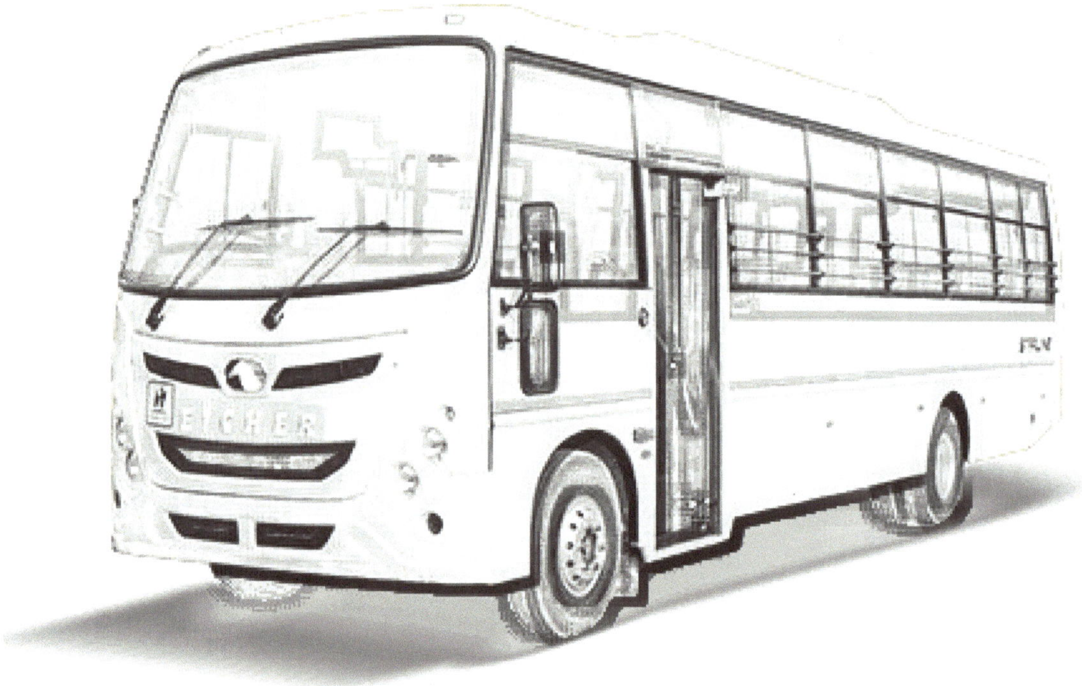
EICHER

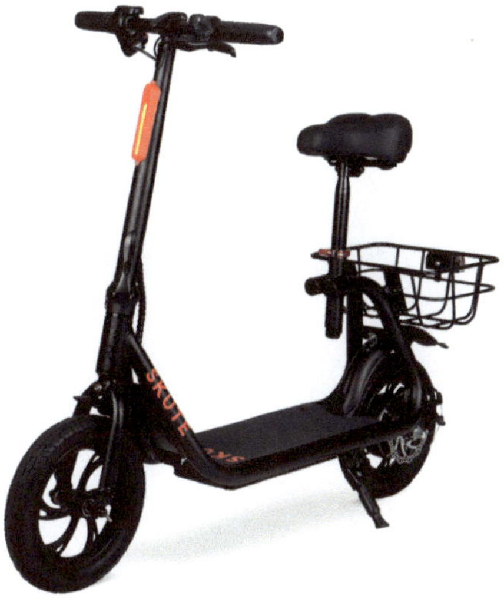
SKUTE

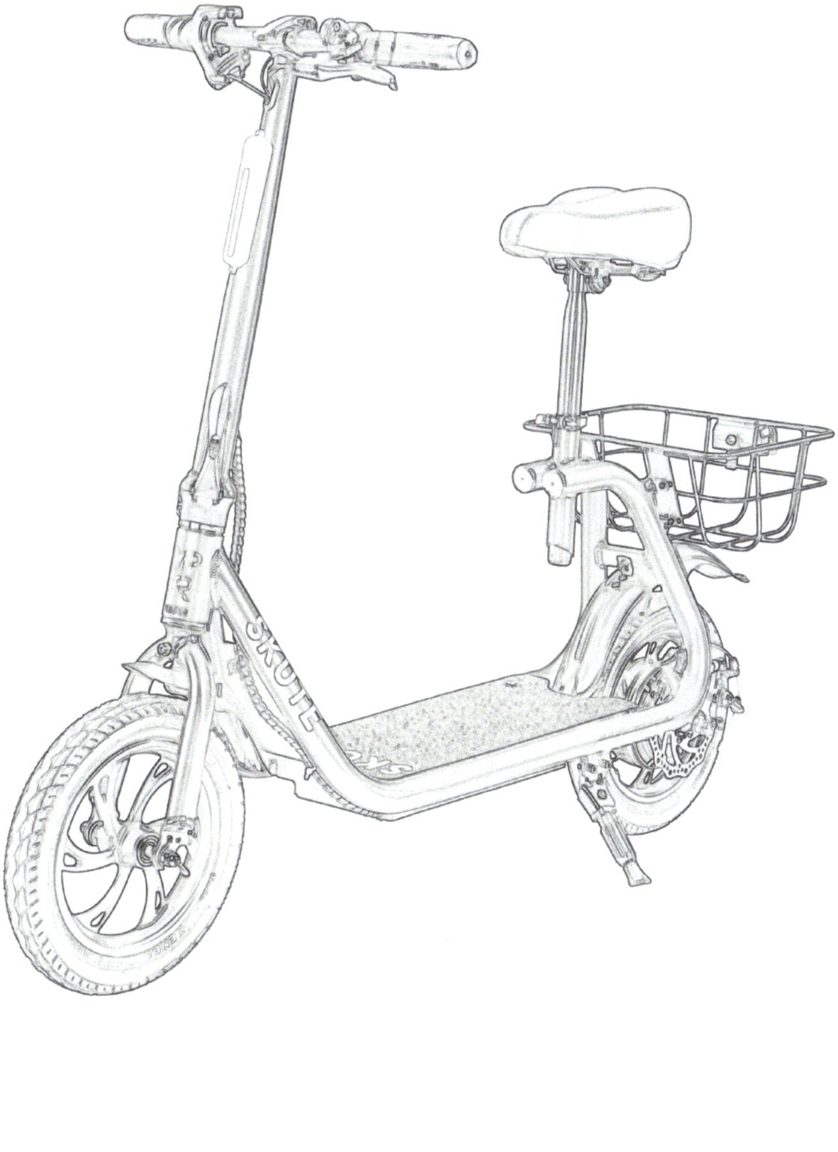
SKUTE

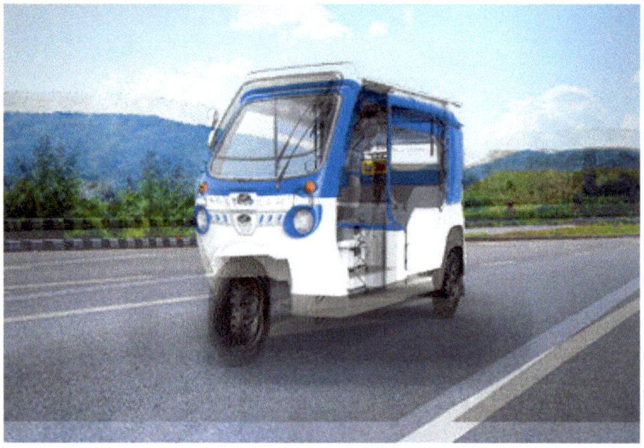

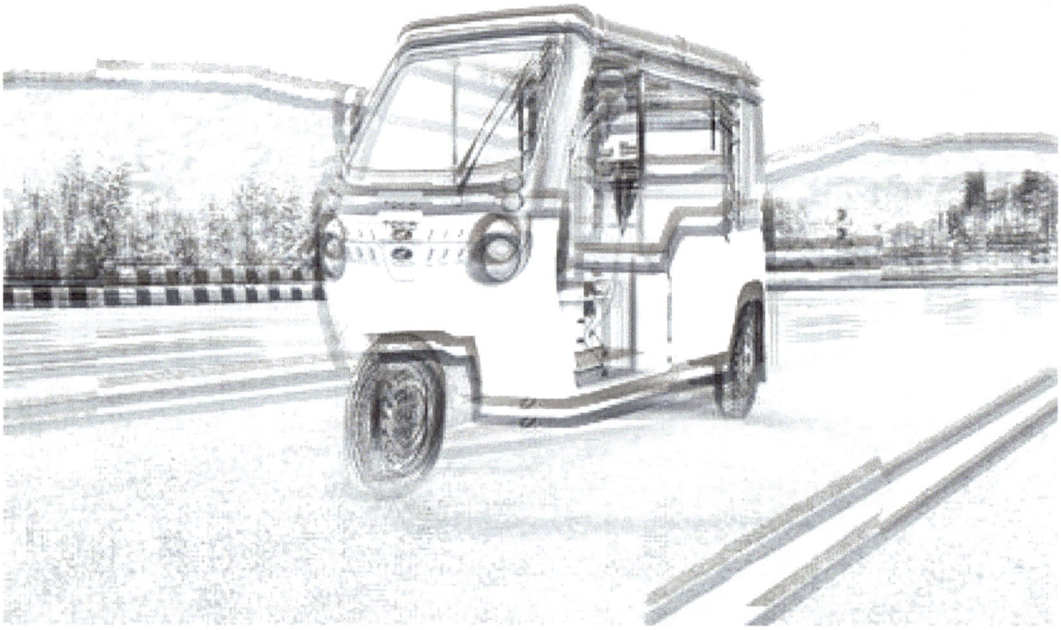

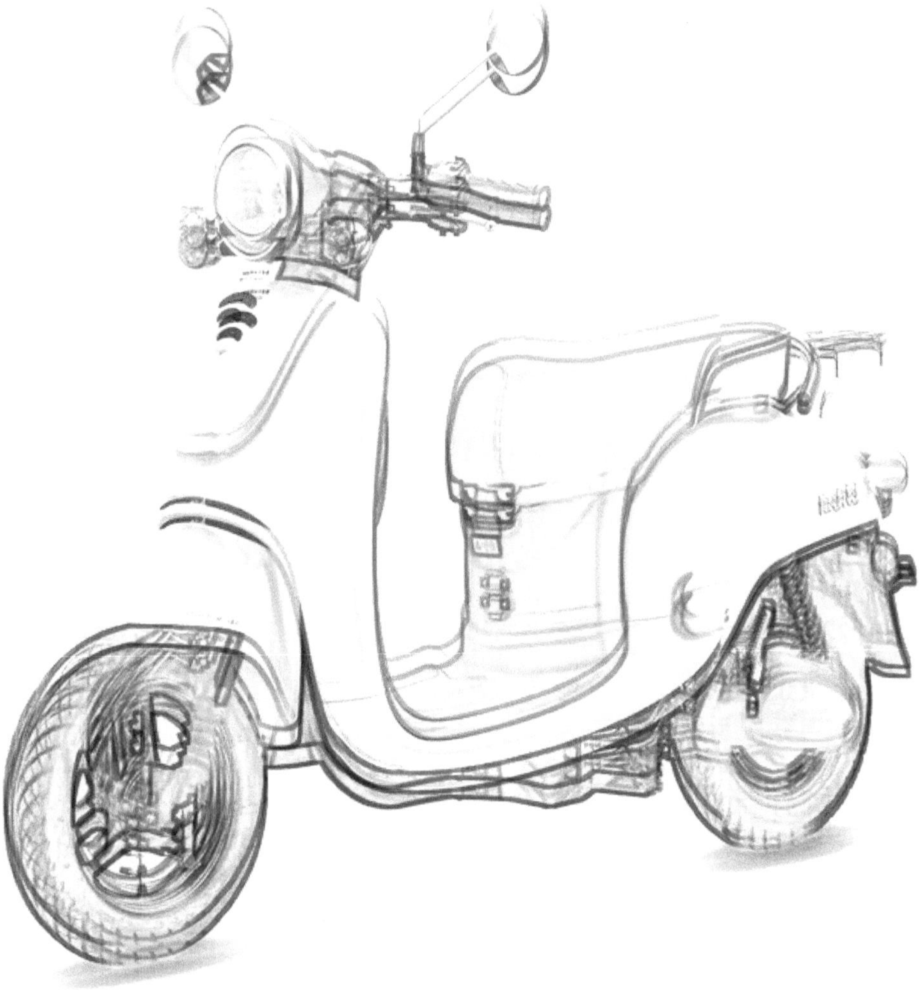

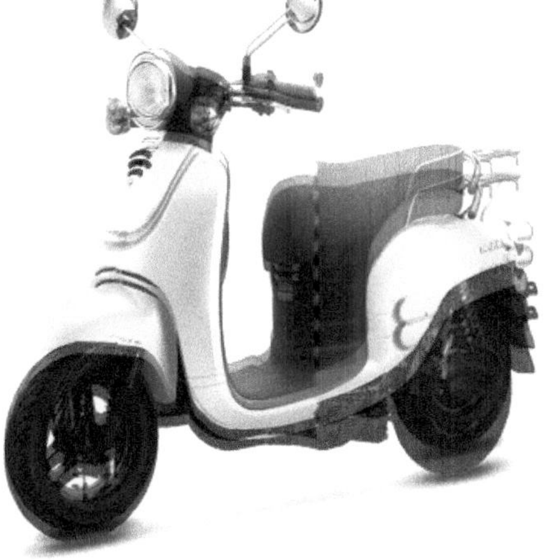

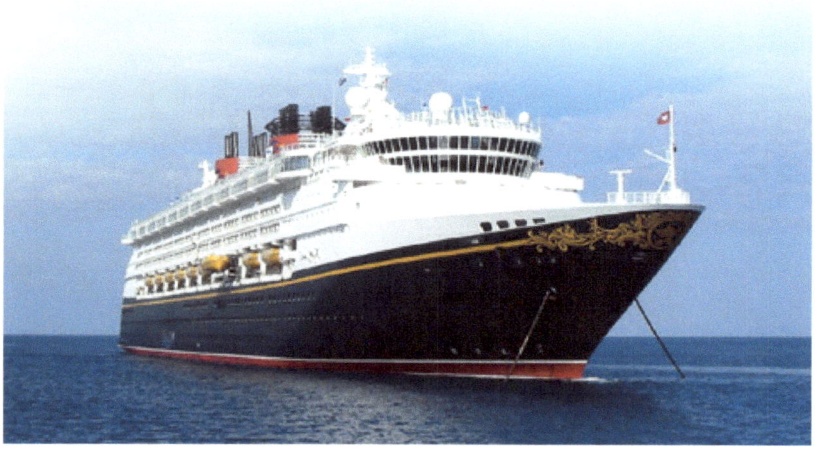

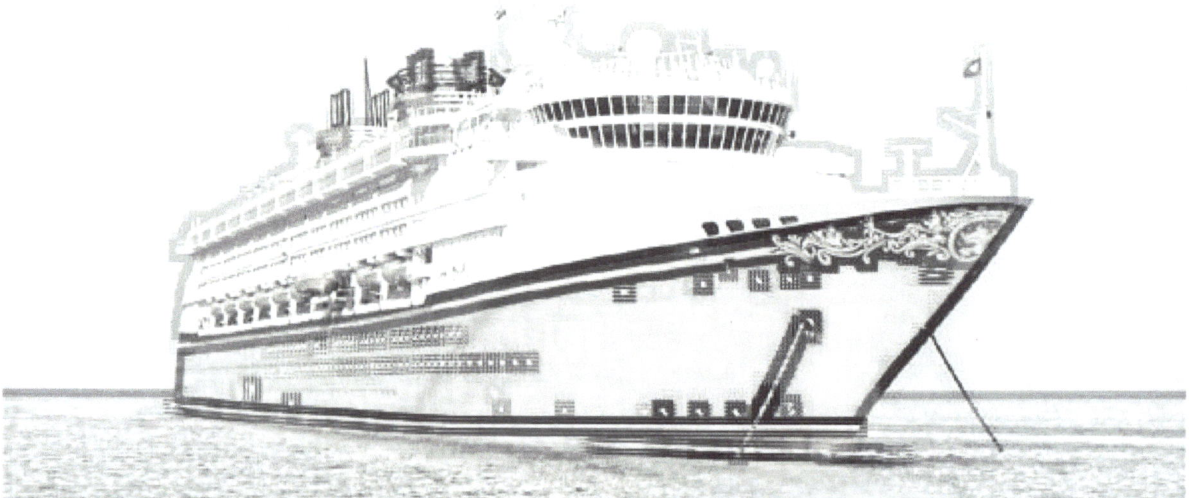

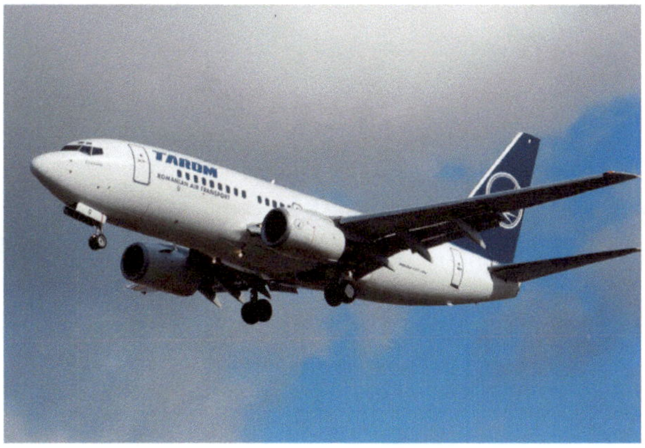
TAROM
ROMANIAN AIR TRANSPORT

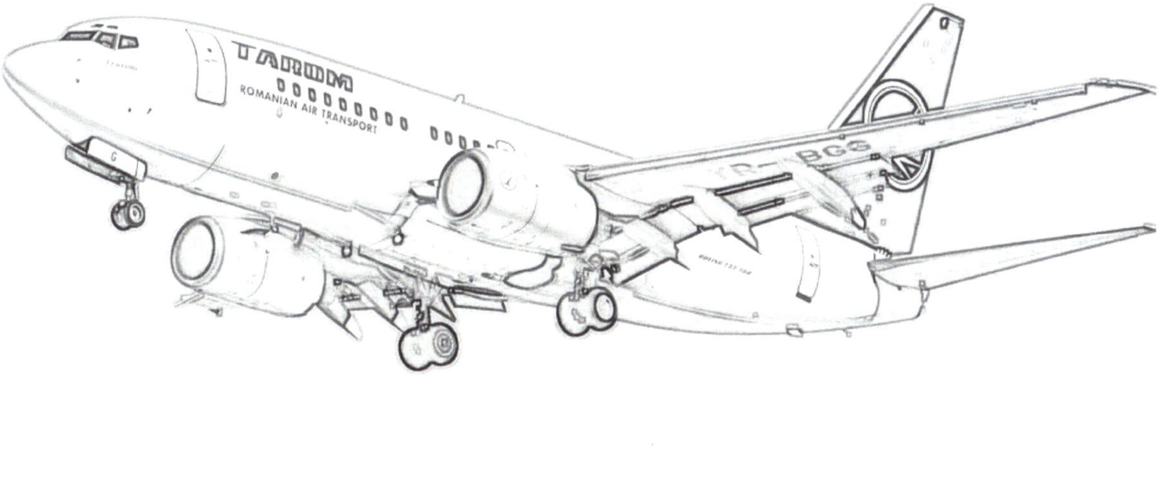
TAROM
ROMANIAN AIR TRANSPORT

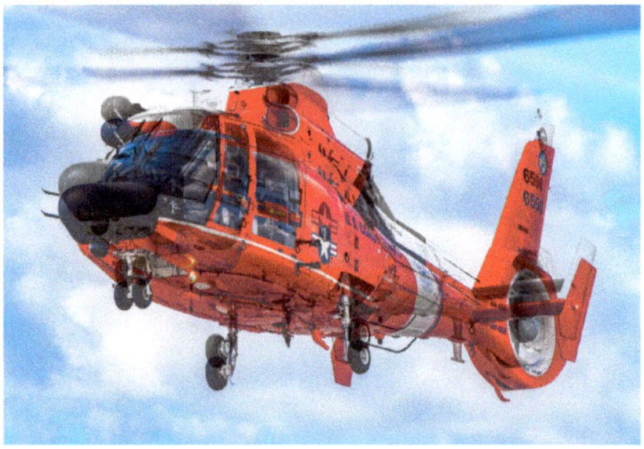

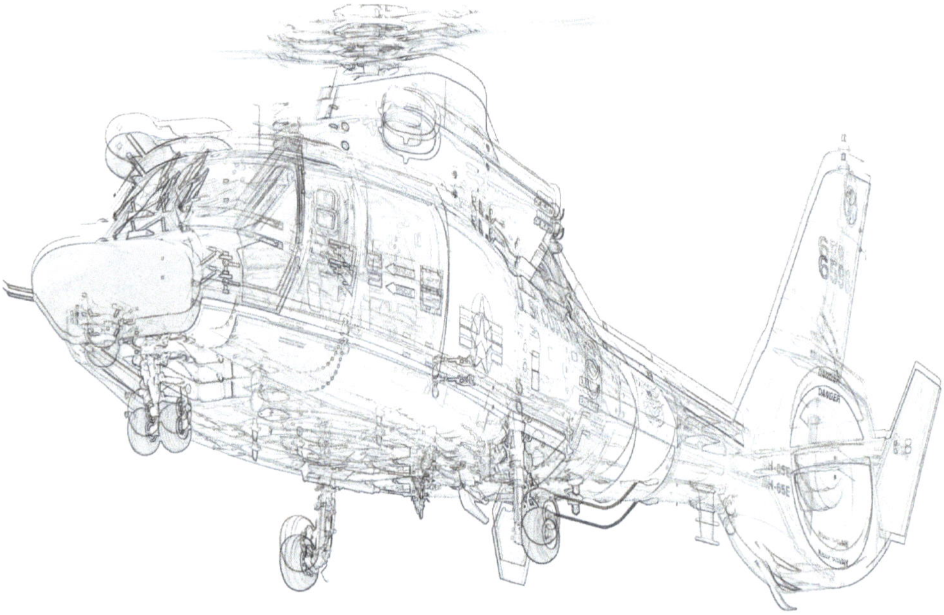
DANGER
H-65E

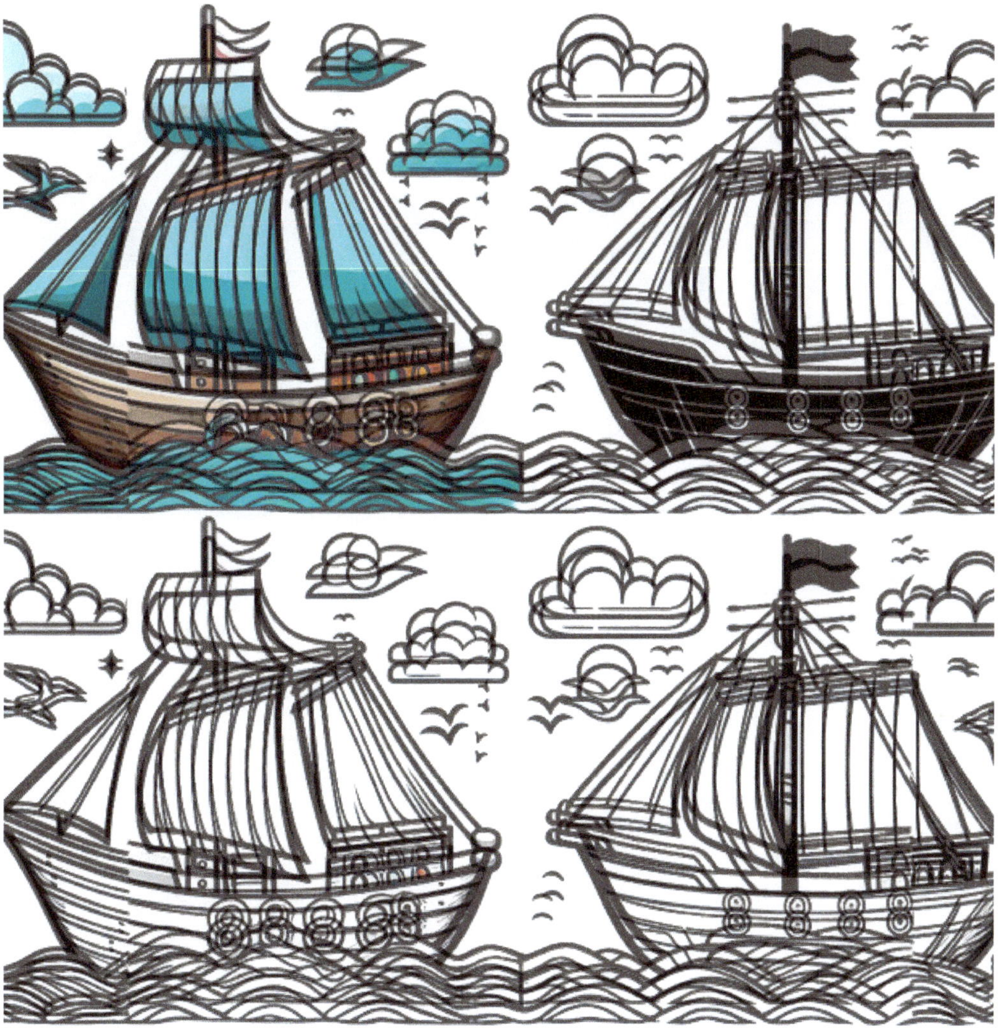

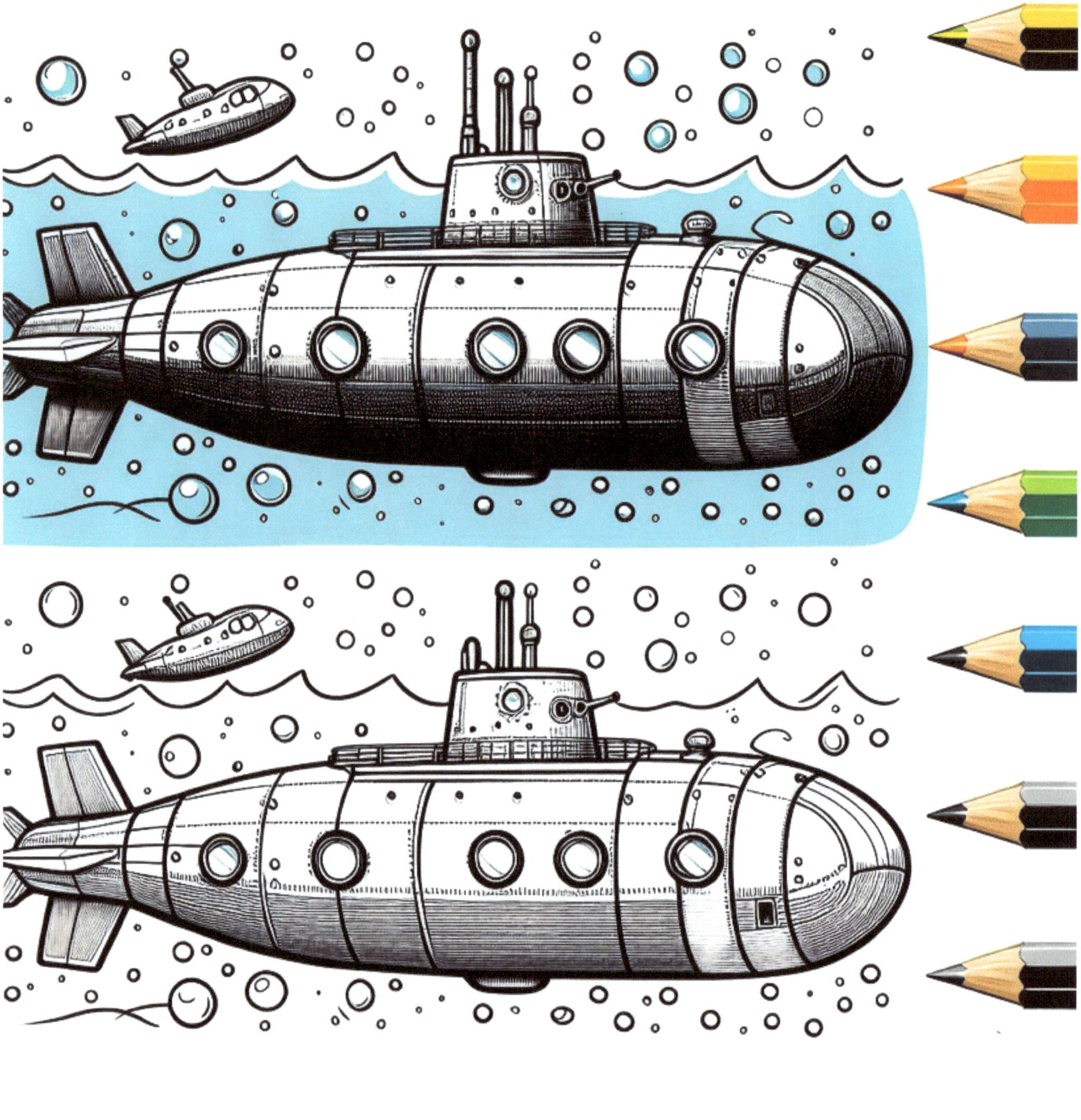

www.ingramcontent.com/pod-product-compliance
Lightning Source LLC
Chambersburg PA
CBHW051944210526
45473CB00006B/2378
* 9 7 9 8 3 2 0 1 3 1 4 8 1 *